To Rhona —

holy cards
dead women talking

May the "she-saints"
bless you!

Penny-Anne

The Black Moss Press First Lines Poetry series is for writers who are publishing their first book of poetry.

Books in the First Lines series include:

Now That We Know Who We Are, by Carlinda D'Alimonte – #1
Moon Sea Crossing, by Lynn Harrison – #2
What Someone Wanted, by Shirley Graham – #3
Swimming in the Dark, by Ross Belot – #4
holy cards: dead women talking, by Penny-Anne Beaudoin – #5

holy
cards
dead women talking

Poems by

Penny-Anne Beaudoin

Black Moss Press
2009

Library and Archives Canada Cataloguing in Publication

Beaudoin, Penny-Anne, 1955-

holy cards : dead women talking / Penny-Anne Beaudoin.

Poems. ISBN 978-0-88753-464-5
    I. Title.
PS8603.E366H65 2009   C811'.6   C2009-902618-X

Cover Image: The Martyrdom of Saint Margaret (detail), fresco,
              1474-79, Saint Margaret Chapel in Crea, Sanctuary
              of Crea (AL), Italy
Cover Design: Karen Veryle Monck

Every effort has been made to secure permission for illustrations
reproduced in this book from the rightful copyright holders. We
regret any inadvertent omission.

Black Moss Press is published at 2450 Byng Road, Windsor, Ontario,
Canada N8W3E8. Black Moss books are distributed in Canada and
the U.S. by LitDistco. All orders should be directed there. Black
Moss can be contacted on its website at www.blackmosspress.com.

Black Moss acknowledges the generous support for its publishing
program from The Canada Council for the Arts and The Ontario
Arts Council.

Le Conseil des Arts | The Canada Council
du Canada | for the Arts

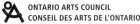

ONTARIO ARTS COUNCIL
CONSEIL DES ARTS DE L'ONTARIO

Acknowledgements

The holy cards St. Joan, St. Irene and St. Agatha appeared in a slightly different form in *The Windsor Review*.

This book would not have been possible without the intercession of many of my very own patron saints. I am indebted to:

Marty Gervais, who brought this work to completion with astonishing speed and amazing grace;

Janine Morris, editor extraordinaire, for her invaluable suggestions regarding the structuring of the book;

Sarah St. Pierre, for her sharp eye and editorial advice;

The Writers' Salon, for their insights and critiques;

M. Norbese Philip for her editorial suggestions;

Sister Mary Joel Zobro, SM, the first to recognize my vocation to the literary life and steadfast champion of my work;

Emmanuelle Vivier, for her friendship, her help with French translations, her gentle editing, and her unflagging belief that this day would come;

Mary Ann Mulhern, whose kind guidance and ebullient encouragement helped transform my timorous journey through the labyrinth of first time publication into a joyous and exciting expedition;

And finally my husband Tony, who years ago took up all the myriad duties of running a household to give me that most precious gift – time to write. To him, my gratitude, my love.

illustrations

St. Joan of Arc
(Artist Unknown. Public Domain.)

8

St. Angela of Foligno
(Artist Unknown. Public Domain.)

20

St. Margaret Mary Alacoque
Contemplating the Sacred Heart of Jesus
(Corrado Giaquinto, c. 1765. Public Domain.)

52

St. Faith
(Artist Unknown.)

78

The Martyrdom of St. Agatha
(Sebastiano del Piombo, 1520. Public Domain.)

108

holy cards

Visionaries

9

Mothers, Wives and Daughters

21

Vowed Religious

53

Martyrs

79

Afterword

109

Visionaries

St. Catherine Labouré
St. Bernadette Soubirous
St. Joan of Arc
St. Catherine of Siena
St. Margaret of Cortona

St. Catherine Labouré

Born 1806 near Dijon, France. Died 1876. Seven months after entering the Daughters of Charity, she said she was awakened in the night by an angel who urged her to go to the chapel as the Virgin Mary was waiting for her. The Virgin gave her several messages over the next three days and commissioned her to have a medal struck, later known as the Miraculous Medal, which would anticipate and popularize the dogma of the Immaculate Conception twenty-four years before it was officially defined. Her body is incorrupt and on display at the Rue de Bac chapel in Paris. Her pictures show her in ecstasy, resting her hands on the Virgin's lap, as she said she did during the first visitation.

i knew they were wrong
the scholars
theologians
learned men
the ones who said
we are born damned
that baptism is a bare remedy
for the primordial sin of man
and no help at all
for the filth and shame
that is woman

i knew it was a lie
        the first instant i gazed into her face
she
of the reasonable eyes
warmth and grace
pulsing from her holy fingernails
i found a friendly space
beneath her mantle
where she held me
and all my sisters
held us precious
cherished

immaculate

St. Bernadette Soubirous

Born 1844, Lourdes, France. Died 1879. At 14, she experienced a series of eighteen visitations from a "beautiful lady" who appeared in a small grotto next to the river Gave. The lady asked Bernadette to have a church built on the site and to "let processions come hither." During the course of the apparitions, the lady directed Bernadette to scratch at the earth, and a spring welled up which is credited over the years with miraculous healings. The lady eventually identified herself as "the Immaculate Conception," a title that caused no small controversy, as the dogma of the Virgin Mary's conception free from original sin had been defined a scant four years earlier, a fact of which Bernadette, who could scarcely read or write, was unaware. The lady made a personal promise to Bernadette that she would not know happiness in this world, but only in the next. Bernadette entered the Convent of St. Girard in Nevers, France in part to escape the constant interrogations of church officials and importuning pilgrims. She died there after a painful illness, at the age of thirty-five. When the cause for her beatification was advanced thirty years later, her body was exhumed and found incorrupt. It is on display at the Convent of St. Girard. Her iconography depicts her as a young girl on her knees in ecstasy before a beautiful lady dressed in white.

no happiness for me
in this world
no healing either
the spring was never meant for me
others would build the church
the learned would debate theology
the wise would determine my significance
and my worthiness

i never cared about any of that

all i ever wanted was
just to look at her
just look at her
just look

St. Joan of Arc

Born circa 1412 in Domrémy, France. Died 1431. When she was about twelve, Joan began having visions of saints Catherine, Margaret and Michael, who urged her to help the then Dauphin Charles reclaim the throne of France. Charles granted her an army which she successfully led to lift the siege of Orléans in 1429, and to several other decisive victories thereafter. Charles was crowned King Charles VII in 1429 and Joan was present at his coronation. She was captured by the Burgundians at Compiègne in 1430, sold to the English and put on trial in a church court. It was the custom of the time for the family of prisoners to ransom them from the enemy, but Joan's family had no money. Charles has been severely criticized for not coming to her aid. She was convicted of heresy based almost entirely on the fact that she had cut her hair and wore men's clothes when she traveled and on the battlefield. She was burned at the stake in 1431. She is nearly always portrayed with short hair, wearing armour and carrying a banner or sword.

cut your hair
wear their clothes
fight their wars
play their games
say their prayers
share their miseries
bring them victories
give them the power they crave

dream with them
weep with them
bleed with them

be one of them
be the best of them

and they'll still
leave you to burn

St. Catherine of Siena

Born 1347, Siena Italy. Died 1380. A Dominican tertiary known for her extreme asceticism, she convinced Pope Gregory XI to leave Avignon and return to Rome, negotiated peace between Rome and Florence, and spent the latter years of her life trying to heal the Great Schism. She experienced the phenomenon of "mystical marriage" to Christ, and in 1375 received the stigmata which, at her request, remained invisible until after her death. Her iconography shows her in ecstasy, receiving her wedding ring from Christ, or the stigmata.

i challenged princes
          and commanded popes
reprimanded queens
chastised the clergy

and made myself throw up
after every meal

i dictated doctrinal treatises
sent letters all over europe
negotiated for peace
counselled the powerful

and whipped myself raw
three times a day

i nursed plague victims and lepers
fed the poor
held the hand of the condemned

and pressed a metal-spiked belt
          around my waist

powerful men tried to kill me once
and i grieved when they did not succeed

i could not eat
i would not sleep
i killed myself daily for my sins

and when my sacred spouse
offered me his stigmata
i begged him let it be invisible
so no one will know
i am a woman
crucified

St. Margaret of Cortona

Born 1247, Tuscany. Died 1297. At age seventeen, she eloped with a young nobleman and lived as his mistress for nine years, during which time she bore him a son. After her lover was murdered, Margaret abandoned his estate and together with her son, presented herself to the Friars Minor at Cortona seeking sanctuary. From then on Margaret undertook a life of good works and austere penance. She is reported to have said to her spiritual director, "My father, do not ask me to give into this body of mine. I cannot afford it. Between me and my body there must needs be a struggle unto death." Her body is incorrupt and lies at St. Basil's Church in Cortona.

it must be broken
this unruly body this
instrument of sin
it must be subjugated
made to atone for

the gorgeous gowns
          with rags
the sumptuous meals
          with starvation fasts
the luxurious feather bed
          with bare ground

the beauty of this face
must be disfigured
these lovely hands
          ruined
these shoulders he once reverenced with his kiss
these shoulders he kissed
these shoulders flayed raw and bloody these shoulders these
shoulders

for herein lies salvation
in the performance and daily repetition of mortifications
until the sin is purged
until this mind can no longer recall the time
when this body was so loved this body
was
so loved

B· ANGELA DE FVLGINIO·

Mothers, Wives and Daughters

St. Cunegundes
St. Maura
St. Margaret Clitherow
St. Margaret the Barefoot
St. Angela of Foligno
St. Laura Vicuña
St. Irene
St. Barbara
St. Dymphna

St. Cunegundes

Born 975 in what is now Germany. Died 1040. Empress of Rome. Her husband, St. Henry II, consented to live with her platonically so she might keep the vow of virginity she had made before their marriage. However, some members of the royal court brought accusations of adultery against Cunegundes, and she was obliged to prove her innocence by walking over red hot ploughshares. Her iconography shows her hiking her skirts to walk barefoot over the glowing metal while Henry and the court look on.

adultery

of all the charges they could have concocted against me
        they had to choose the most absurd
i laughed so uproariously
        it took me a moment to realize
        i was laughing alone

henry stared at me
        and the doubt in his eyes
        brought tears to my own

oh henry, you can't possibly believe…

but i should have known better
a man's infidelity must always be excused
while a woman's fidelity must always be proved

very well
what evidence would satisfy the court?
i had thought
        naively it turns out
an examination by the court physician would suffice

but no
the council was in the mood for something
        a trifle more biblical

i must walk
unharmed
over molten metal

if my feet remained intact
　　　　then apparently so was my hymen

again i looked to henry
again he just stared back

right to the last second i thought
　　　　he would defend me
　　　　protect me
　　　　at least believe me

i removed my slippers and stockings
and thought
darling henry
you will hate yourself forever because of this

24

i ignored his uncertain eyes
　　　　his quickened breath as i
strode without hesitation
onto the fiery floor

and *danced*

twirled
spun myself this way and that
kicked up my delicate white heels
　　　　at the slavering courtiers

then i curtsied to the throne
        my petticoats beginning to smolder
and extended my hand
to the red-faced king

henry, i called
darling
won't you join me?

St. Maura

Date of birth uncertain. Died 286, Egypt. Twenty days after their wedding, Maura's husband Timothy was arrested and brought before Arianus, governor of Thebes on the charge of possessing Christian Scriptures. When he refused to surrender the holy texts, the governor subjected him to various tortures and then had Maura brought to the prison to see if her presence might weaken her husband's resolve. She tried to persuade him to obey the governor, but he encouraged her not to fear martyrdom. Thereupon she confessed her faith and told her husband, "I am prepared to die with you." Arianus proceeded to torture Maura as well, tearing out her hair and cutting off her fingers. At last he had them both crucified, facing one another. They survived on their crosses for nine days.

near the end
language failed
dialogue dissolved in the fetid air between us

then my body became a lexicon
the flesh became word

when i arched towards him
straining against the nails in the stumps of my hands
it meant
i wish i could touch you

when i twisted my decaying limbs heaved
my labouring chest groaned
in all my inward parts
it was a prayer
to god
to be merciful
to my husband
grant him peace
end his suffering
do it now

and my eyes
my relentless gaze
filled with the fierceness of a woman dying
in love
fixed on his ravaged face
never wavering
not for one moment not
for one instant though
seven days should turn to eight
or nine
or ten

it's how i held him
told him
i'm here
i'm here
no, timothy, look
i'm here

St. Margaret Clitherow

Born 1556, England. Died 1586. Arrested for sheltering priests in her home and organizing Masses for the Catholic underground community. She refused to enter a plea at her trial to spare her husband and children the danger of testifying, and was summarily sentenced to death by pressing. She was laid on a sharp rock, a board placed on top of her, and heavier and heavier weights were added until her ribs were crushed and she died of suffocation. It is reported she lasted only fifteen minutes.

29

as if i had a choice
as if there was any alternative

what was i to do?
i could not even plead ignorance of god's will
no, i knew only too well what he required of me
and once knowing
            what help was there but to obey?

it has ever been thus
when the path before me was clear and certain
            some almighty force compelled me to walk in it
heedless of the cost
            my children's shattered looks
            my husband's broken heart

the court was surprised
            i endured a scant quarter of an hour
but you see
            god
had been pressing down on me for years

such a relief
            to finally get *that* off my chest

St. Margaret the Barefoot

Born 1325, San Severino, Italy. Died, 1395. Married at fifteen. Endured years of abuse at the hand of her husband who was particularly incensed by Margaret's attachment to the Church and her charity to the poor.

i was poor
and uneducated
but i understood
the requirements of sanctity

i must forgive
i must be patient
i must forgive
i must endure

i could not defend myself
i could not leave him
i could not hide
i could not ask anyone for help
i could not ask him to stop

i was left with my prayers
and one disturbing
recurring
dream

two small hands
clenched into fists
hitting and
hitting and
hitting

back

St. Angela of Foligno (blessed)

Born 1248, Foligno, Italy. Died 1309. Nicknamed "The Swooning Saint" after a spectacular and public conversion experience at the basilica in Assisi. Prayed for the deaths of her children, husband, and mother that she might be free to pursue her religious inclinations. All of them died within a year. She wrote: "Because I had already entered the aforesaid way, and had prayed to God for their death, I felt a great consolation when it happened." She joined the Third Order of St. Francis and became one of the foremost Franciscan theologians and mystics. She is depicted in ecstasy before a vision of Christ.

33

you cut a wide and merciless swath to reach me
        didn't you, lover?
slaughtered every member of my family
and all because
i asked you to

so many funerals
so few tears
for with the growing silence
        as one by one they fell
i had to fight to still my singing heart
        my thrilling spirit

oh, how i rejoice in thee, o christ
and praise thy mighty works!

no more
        mewling, puling, bawling, squalling little mouths
silenced for good
        the nagging, ragging, harping, carping of eternal
maternal advice
gone forever
        the smothering obesity
        the slobbering indecency
that crawled atop me night after night
        to murder my passion
        strangle my affection
        crush the life out of me

all gone
everyone
every impediment
that caused me to offer up
my horrible homicidal petitions

...which you saw fit to answer, o christ
      with what can only be described as
      a shameless expediency

so don't even think of playing the gentle saviour with me
      jesus, meek and lowly
i watched you stride knee-deep through gore
      kicking aside the bodies of my children
      to get to me
so no pious pretense, if you please
i know what you are
same as me
the two of us
      unhinged
      by the savage excesses of love

now tell me
      my beloved assassin
shall we go to your father
take a knee before his throne
confess our...indiscretion
and beg to be clothed in the sweet reasonable
      cooling grace of heaven

or

shall we join our bloody hands together
and naked
leap laughing
into the frenzied flames of hottest hell

you decide

St. Laura Vicuña (blessed)

Born 1891, Santiago, Chile. Died 1904, Las Lajas, Argentina. After her father's death, her destitute mother fled to Argentina where she became the mistress of a wealthy landowner, Manuel Mora. Laura thrived at school, but when she returned home to visit, Mora made advances on her, and physically abused her mother. Sometime later, Laura received permission from her confessor to offer her life for her mother's salvation. Soon after, she became seriously ill and had to return home to her mother's care. In a drunken rage, Mora once again threatened her and then beat her unconscious. She died eight days later after telling her mother of her prayer. After Laura's death, her mother left Mora, and returned to the church. The fate of Manuel Mora remains unclear.

if i had been born
        a boy
things would have been different

if i had had fists
        instead of breasts
i'd have made him pay
        for what he did to my mother
        for every mark he left on her body
        for the repeated rape of her soul

but i was a girl
        and a good girl at that

good girls don't fight
        they're beaten
good girls don't kill
        they're martyred

mama received no justice
        against the rich man who took my life
the priests said
        be happy your child's a saint
and she smiled
because she was a good girl too

but after those holy men glided away
        trailing their pious consolations behind them
her smile
failed
and she
fell
to the floor
hemorrhaging shrieks and curses

St. Irene

Third century saint. Widow of the martyr St. Castulus. Nursed St. Sebastian back to health after he was shot with arrows and left for dead. According to the legend, after Sebastian was finally martyred circa 288, Irene was charged with possessing Scriptures, a capital offence under the Emperor Diocletian. She refused to sacrifice to the gods, and was ordered into a house of prostitution. Emerging unharmed, she was executed, ironically, by an arrow through the throat. She is almost always pictured with St. Sebastian.

he hated me for saving him
in his eyes
        an unforgivable sin

the way he shrieked as i cut him down
stop! stop! what are you doing? you'll ruin everything!

sebastian, i explained
your archers have bungled the job
you bristle like a porcupine
        but your martyrdom is incomplete
not one of your wounds is mortal
i could leave you here another week
        with no fear of you dying

leave me anyway! he pleaded
maybe they'll come back
or maybe some wild beast of the forest...

no, my dear
you'll just have to accept the fact
        heaven doesn't want you yet

all the way home he grumbled in my ear
robbed! i've been robbed! cheated of my crown!
i trained those archers myself
        so where did they learn such ineptitude?
perhaps if i had drawn a bull's-eye on my chest for them...

i tried to comfort
tried to soothe
you'll have better luck next time, dear

perhaps the emperor will hire a foreign marksman
     i hear the french have deadly aim
you know he will not rest until your heart is pierced
     and you are mouldering in your grave

you think so? he asked
     his face lit with pathetic hope

without a doubt

i dragged him to my home
plucked out his arrows like feathers off a chicken
sewed him up with needle and thread
     making a patchwork of scars on his smooth-muscled chest
     all crooked seams
     the kind my mother would have scolded me for
fed him by my own hand
warmed him in my own bed
anointed his wounds with wine and oil
     and holy kisses
and knew a happiness i hadn't felt
     since before my own husband washed his robes
     in the blood of the lamb

with time
his young body healed
and i hoped his madness too had passed
but one night
while i sewed
and i thought he dozed by the fire
he startled me saying
the emperor will pass through the city
     tomorrow afternoon

i knew instantly what he was thinking
what he was planning to do
my hands trembled
but i kept my voice steady
sebastian dear
won't you stay with me?
would that not please you?
think of all we could do together
work and pray
worship and love
we could raise chickens
plant rosebushes
put up preserves
maybe have a child or two

i glanced at his profile
then back to my sewing

we could move away from this troubled place
find a peaceful home
put fear in the closet
learn to laugh at the rain
teach our children happy songs

i leaned over
touched his arm

put aside this lust for death
our god cannot be
        nearly so bloodthirsty
surely he is as pleased with holy living
        as holy dying

stay with me
darling sebastian
stay and be happy

he said nothing for a long moment
and the weight of his silence
        smothered the tiny bird
        singing within me
in his eyes
a familiar fire burned

so it's true what they say
he snarled at last
the devil does appear
        as an angel of light!

he cast off his covers
jumped to his feet

this bed is too soft
this cabin too warm
i've dallied here long enough
and you... he shook his finger at me
you would keep me from my sacred mission
distract me from my reward
with your soft lips and
warm arms and
talk of homes and children and love
you dishonour the memory of your martyr-husband
you dishonour yourself!
suffering
pain

the royal road of the cross
that is the only way to glory!
get thee behind me satan!
i'll hear no more of your seductions!
your talk of chickens and roses!
on
on to meet my destiny
on to meet my lord!

so he's off now
to find someone
anyone he can goad
      into giving him what he wants most
a baptism of blood
a holy killing
a righteous assassination
and the bloodier the better

fine

but i swear
if they botch the job again
this time
i'll finish him off myself

St. Barbara

Martyred in the early third century. According to legend, she was born to a pagan father who shut her up in a tower to keep her away from would-be suitors. He became enraged when she converted to Christianity and dragged her before the Roman prefect who ordered her tortured and beheaded. Her father is supposed to have carried out the execution himself. She is the only saint portrayed carrying a chalice and host, the sacramental signs of Christ's body and blood.

I

daddy is very happy

he's built me a tower to live in

says to think of the walls
      like his arms
      wrapped around me
      forever and
      ever and
      ever
protecting me
      from evil
saving me
      from the harm
      men would do to me

my daddy
      is all love

II

daddy is very angry

calls me stupid
     for falling in love
     with a dead man

says i've betrayed him
     with my crucified lover

i have cracked the hourglass
and his love for me
has all run out

hands me over
     to the men he once
     shielded me from
and watches
     wide-eyed
every torment
every humiliation

asks for
begs for
insists on
     the honour
of hacking off my head
while i still breathe

has to wipe the slobber
     off his mouth
when they hand him the sword

III

our bodies
            broken
our blood
            spilled
but look jesus
our daddies
            are happy
once again

St. Dymphna

Seventh century saint. Daughter of a pagan Irish chieftain and Christian mother. Legend has it her mother died when Dymphna was fourteen. Her father scoured the territory for a replacement matching his wife's beauty. When none was found, his counsellors suggested he marry his own daughter. After spurning her father's advances, Dymphna fled with her spiritual advisor, Father Gerebernus to Gheel, Belgium. Through his spies and informants, her father tracked her down, murdered the priest and then beheaded his daughter when she refused to return to Ireland with him.

48

god is very fond of dead virgins
        father gerebernus told me one day when we were in
hiding

dead virgins?

that's right
especially those who die violently
        in defence of their virginity
why, when those blessed women arrive at the gates of paradise
        all the angel host sing their praises throughout the
heavenly courts

i see, i said
and those virgins who die of natural causes?

uh, well, of course the angels sing for them too
        but not as loudly
so, if your father should ever find you
        not only must you prevent him
        from destroying your precious virginity
but it would be best if you could get him
        to kill you as well

but what if i want to live?

how's that?

live, father
i'm only fourteen
what if i want to live?
is life not as precious as virginity?

no
no it's not
think about it dymphna
if you submit to your father
        you won't be a virgin
and what's more, you won't be dead
what will the angels have to sing about then?

i see, i said again
but what if i only pretend to submit?

how's that?

pretend, father
what if i return to my home
        as my father wishes
lie down on mama's side of the bed
but slip a little knife under the wedding pillow
and what if
i use that little knife to still my father's raging heart
        before he can touch me
would that not be the best alternative of all?

that's murder, dymphna

it's murder if *he* kills *me*
but if *i* take *his* life
      he is prevented from committing murder
      he is prevented from committing incest
i preserve my life
      my precious virginity
and i send my father straight to heaven
      which would seem to me to be the only way
      he's ever going to get there
is that not an act
      of salvation?

gerebernus opened his mouth
      as if to say something
then closed it with a snap
he blinked his hawkish eyes at me
      once
      twice
      thrice
then shook himself all over and said

      let's not confuse the angels
         shall we?

Vowed Religious

St. Margaret Mary Alacoque
St. Jeanne Louise Barré
St. Isidora the Simple
St. Marie-Thèrése Haze
Sts. Catherine of Pallanza and Juliana Puricelli
St. Ebba
St. Imelda
St. Teresa of Avila
St. Marina

St. Margaret Mary Alacoque

Born 1647 in what is now east central France. Died 1690. Took a vow of chastity at the age of four. Entered the Order of the Visitation when she was 24. There she received a series of visions of Christ who chose her as his disciple to propagate devotion to the Sacred Heart. Though she faced much initial resistance, she had the satisfaction of seeing the Church authenticate her visions and establish the devotion before she died. Her mystical experiences drove her to what one commentator described as "appalling austerities," and were a constant source of disruption to her community. She wrote: "He enkindled therein such an ardent desire to love Him and to suffer that I no longer had any rest. He pursued me so closely that I had no leisure except to think of how I could love Him by crucifying myself." She is depicted in ecstasy before a vision of Christ, his wounded heart exposed.

the sisters took to squirting holy water on me
        whenever they passed me in the hallway
they thought me possessed

they weren't far wrong

he addicted me
        to the taste of his flesh
        melting on my tongue
his blood
        trickling down my throat
he ripped out my heart
        left a searing flame in its place
so every moment of every day
i would burn for him

he led me into temptation
seduced me to the dark music of crucifixion
left me panting
        in sweats of blood
battered
laid open
gutted like a fish

and with every crushing blow
        every stinging laceration
        the slow evisceration
i sang alleluia
alleluia
alleluia

St. Jeanne Louise Barré (blessed)

Born 1750 in Ostrevent, France. Martyred 1794 in Valencienes. Ursuline lay sister. When the sisters at the convent were arrested during the French Revolution for operating a parochial school and teaching Catholicism, Sr. Barré was somehow overlooked. But as they were being carted off to the guillotine, she identified herself as one of them and joined them in their martyrdom.

i could have danced naked on the altar
and their only reaction would have been
        how did the altar cloths
        get so wrinkled?

they didn't see me
never noticed me
but without me
        they wouldn't have survived a week

i was
the lay sister

it fell to me to perform all the tasks
        too menial
for my professed sisters

i worked in their garden
cooked their meals
washed their dishes
made their beds
even emptied their sanctified chamber pots

i'm convinced they thought
        clean socks and underwear
        just appeared in their drawers
        by an act of divine intervention
they certainly never gave me a sign
        they thought i had anything to do with it

and i wasn't asking them
        to kneel down and kiss my feet
ah non!

just a nod
a kind smile
a whispered thank you

just give me a reason
              not to spit in your soup today

non, all i ever got
              was reverend mother's
              unending litany of rules
              for the lay sister

the lay sister does not take her meals
              with the professed sisters
she can eat
in the kitchen

the lay sister does not sing the liturgy of the hours
              with the professed sisters
she can say her prayers
in the kitchen

the lay sister does not share the dormitory
              with the professed sisters
she can sleep
in the kitchen

they even got themselves arrested
              without me

trundled past me in their cart
              noses in the air
oh, look at us everyone

on our way to get our heads chopped off
see you in heaven
if you get that far
which you probably won't
but we will
because we are
- how do you say? -
holier than thou

that was the last straw

i forced my way through the crowd
        and stopped the cart
        with a look so fierce
the horses reared back in terror

had to haul myself over the side
        because of course
no one was going to lend me a hand

and there was reverend mother
        wrinkling up her nose
        as much as to say
isn't there a separate cart
        for the lay sister?

pas cette fois, ma mère

not this time

St. Isidora the Simple

Dates uncertain. Lived at the convent in Tabennis, Egypt. Wore a dishrag on her head as a veil. Considered ignorant and simpleminded by her sisters, she was assigned the most menial chores and was often the butt of their jokes. A hermit, St. Pitirim was compelled by a vision to visit the convent where he was told he would find "an elect vessel full of the grace of God" whom he would identify by a crown shining above her head. When he pointed out Isidora as the fulfillment of the vision, the other nuns immediately changed their attitude and revered her as a living saint in their midst. She ran away in the night to escape their adulation and lived out the rest of her life as a hermitess.

it was a joke
you'll never convince me
　　　that pitirim intended it as anything but a joke

as i tried to explain to my ever-so-clever sisters
he was just being silly
but they wouldn't listen to me
so great was his power over them
　　　if he had pointed to the convent goat
and said, behold the elect vessel of god's grace
i have no doubt but they would have done their best
　　　to try and canonize that poor dumb animal as well

then the fawning
　　　and the flattery
　　　and the slobbering all over me

i will wash sister isidora's veil!
i will wash her feet!
i will clip her toenails!
i will eat them as holy communion!

i fled to my cell but they all stood outside
　　　and sang vespers to me
until i threw my boot at the door
and yelled at them, the living saint in your midst commands
you to go to bed!

a few days later
i escaped through my window
never to return
leaving them to argue about
　　　which of them i loved the best

and they called *me* simpleminded

St. Marie-Thèrése Haze (blessed)

Born 1782, Belgium. Died 1876. Founded the Daughters of the Cross originally to educate the children of the poor. But in 1841, the government convinced her to assume management of a notorious women's prison and then a beggar's prison. After successfully turning around both institutions, she opened The Refuge, a shelter for prostitutes, and it was the residents of The Refuge who ultimately came to the sisters' aid when they were called on to expand their ministry to the victims of typhoid, smallpox and cholera.

it was the whores who saved us

we asked the rich to help
they gave us money
and sent us on our way

we asked the righteous to help
and they promised to pray for us

the whores showed up
an army of them
sleeves rolled back
long hair pinned up
ready to do anything we asked

many of them already carried their own death   63
festering between their legs
but they were fearless
entering plague houses
washing the dead
nursing the dying
gathering up the children in their arms
crooning lullabies
rocking them to sleep

in the coming weeks
as we worked together side by side
my nuns and i kept forgetting
kept calling them
sister

Sts. Catherine of Pallanza
and Juliana Puricelli (blesseds)

Juliana Puricelli (1427-1501) came from a poor family and worked harvesting cotton. After years of abuse at the hands of her father for her refusal to marry, she ran away to a hermitage on Italy's Monte Varese. Catherine of Pallanza (1437-1478) had already been living there for two years, after her wealthy family had been wiped out by the plague. Four more women eventually joined them, and they formed a community under the rule of St. Augustine, although the convent was apparently the subject of much gossip among the townspeople. Catherine, who was greatly devoted to the Passion of Christ, died uttering the words – "I see my beloved Crucified One." There is at least one depiction of Catherine and Juliana together, their eyes raised in prayer, a small angel presenting them with lilies, the symbol of virginity.

i was sixteen when she came to me
blackened eyes
broken body
dragging weights of sorrow and despair up the mountainside

though she was the eldest
          she knelt before me
i am weary of fathers, she said

i tipped up her face to the sky
see how the virgin's sacred mantle is spread over us, i said
beneath it together we'll find ourselves
          a home

never again did she speak
          of the anguish that brought her to me
and her bruises and scars faded
          with the passing of the years
but i knew
          she carried secret wounds
          that bled and bled
          a passiontide
and i prayed god every day
          magnify my heart
          that i might love her more

others joined us
          but she remained the first

i rejoiced when i knew for certain i was dying
          for it meant
i would not have to live a single day
          without her

at the end
          they all pressed around my bed
praying
weeping
hoping for a holy word they could keep eternal

mother, tell us what you see

i searched the throng of faces
          until i found hers
          and blessed it with my eyes
i see my beloved crucified one
          i told them
and while the others sang hymns of praise to god
she bowed her head
          and smiled

St. Ebba

Ninth century saint of royal birth. Became abbess of Coldingham Monastery in England. According to one early chronicler, Ebba and her nuns, to avoid being raped by the invading Danes, mutilated their faces, cutting off their noses and upper lips "to the teeth." Apparently this stratagem was successful: the nuns were not violated, but they were burned alive when the Danes razed the monastery to the ground. St. Ebba is portrayed wearing a crown and holding a staff and sword.

on the last day of my life
        i carried no staff
        i owned no sword
but i took a knife from the kitchen
gathered my sisters around me
and showed them
how to disfigure themselves
if they would remain whole

cut
        i told them
like this
until the bones show through
white and glistening
cut, sisters
cut

and the knife went hand to hand

lips severed
we could no longer speak
but our raw wounds
our blood-soaked robes
bore eloquent testimony

the men
could not hold their stomachs
ran back outside
slammed shut the door

never
was a fire kindled with such haste

quick! quick!
blot it out
burn it down
bury it deep
before the vision can touch you
before it can take hold of your mind

our particulate bodies rose up on the warm air
then drifted down on our brothers
in sooty benediction

we melted into their skin
choked the lice in their hair
slipped into their dry tear ducts
and swam the rivers beneath their tongues

we rode with them for days
lived with them for years
and in the end
we did lie down with them
under the earth's heavy hand
in a quiet slow commingling of
ashes to ashes
dust to dust

St. Imelda Lambertini (blessed)

Born 1322, Bologna, Italy. Died 1333. Devout child of nobility, she received her parents' permission to enter a local Dominican convent at the age of nine. She earnestly desired to receive communion, but at that time, first communicants were required to be fourteen years old. According to her story, on May 12th 1333, after Mass, when she was alone in the chapel, a host miraculously floated from the tabernacle over to where she knelt and hovered just above her. The sister sacristan came upon the scene and hastened to bring a priest, who placed the host on Imelda's tongue. She was left alone to make her thanksgiving, but when she continued to delay in chapel, her sisters returned to find her dead, still kneeling in her place. Her body is incorrupt and on display at the Church of San Sigismondo in Bologna.

thy passion, o christ
is a killing thing
stilling the heart
paralyzing the brain

i took your body within mine
o bread of angels
an innocent consummation
but you
       devoured my spirit
in a red-hot engulfment that
ripped the breath from my lungs

yet be at peace, o lord of life
i hold no rancour

for even had i known
death
was the price of ecstasy
even so
would i have closed my eyes
parted my lips
whispered amen

St. Teresa of Avila

Born 1515, Avila Spain. Died 1582. Reformer of the Carmelite Order and Doctor of the Church. Upon exhumation of her body in 1583, she was found incorrupt, but was almost immediately carved up for relics, many of which are still on display at various churches throughout Spain.

72

for some reason
men just adored my hands
once i was dead

my confessor and friend
padre gracian
dear sweet foolish man
was so overcome
at the sight
of my incorrupt body
he could not restrain himself
but whipped out his saw
and proceeded to lop off my hand
to bring back to my convent in avila, he said
but before it arrived
he'd snipped off the pinky
to keep for himself
wore it around his neck
every day
for the rest of his life
just couldn't live without me
i suppose

and my other hand
by hook or crook
machinations divine
or infernal
ended up at the bedside
of generalissimo franco
right there
between the case that held his glasses
and the glass that held his teeth

every night
after his wife
had surrendered herself
to sleep's sweet oblivion
he would turn his back
on her living flesh
and whisper to my desiccated digits
buenas noches, querida mia
and i
never one to scorn the sinner
would twiddle my fingers back at him
like an old friend
waving
in the dark

St. Marina

Sixth century saint. Born in Lebanon. Disguised herself as a man to live at a monastery. Her brother monks discovered she was a woman only after her death. Her story notwithstanding, she is frequently depicted in feminine robes.

75

a dying brother
once told me
brother marina
your tender care of me
makes me feel
like god himself
is standing at my bedside

i had only moments
before he was beyond hearing
so i
leaned in close and
whispered in his ear

then your god
has breasts

Martyrs

St. Elizabeth Feodorovna
St. Febronia
St. Columba of Sens
St. Maria Goretti
St. Faith
Sts. Justa and Rufina
St. Felicity
St. Edith Stein
St. Lucy
Sts. Valentina and Thea

St. Elizabeth Feodorovna

Born 1864, Germany. Died 1918, Russia. German princess married to Grand Duke Sergei Alexandrovich of Russia. After her husband's assassination in 1905, she dismissed her court, and founded the convent of Sts. Martha and Mary, where she oversaw a ministry to the poor and sick, and abandoned children. In 1918, during the Russian Revolution, she was taken from her convent and put under arrest with other members of the royal family. They were taken to an abandoned iron mine, and thrown down the shaft one at a time, beginning with Elizabeth. According to the testimony of one of the assassins, the victims all survived the fall as they were able to hoist themselves out of the pool of water at the bottom of the shaft onto a small ledge. Even after two hand grenades had been tossed in after them, their voices could still be heard raised in song. In a desperate attempt to complete the botched assassinations, the shaft was filled with brush and set afire. It appears the victims all died of asphyxiation. St. Elizabeth is canonized in the Russian Orthodox Church.

we sang

from the bottom of the pit
bodies broken
we found our breath
and sang

a hymn from the heart of hell
lord, save your people
save your people, o lord

a grenade
whistled down the mineshaft
then another
and still

we sang
reaching for each other's hands
in the ringing darkness

our assassins were appalled
shut them up, for god's sake!
for god's sake, shut them up!

baptism to cremation
genesis to apocalypse
water to fire
and smothering smoke
then at last
the silence they craved

years later
when the madness had subsided
and our killers had slipped back
to their normal lives
quiet farms
loving families
and atrocities and massacres
barely rippled the surface of their dreams
now and then
they would find themselves
humming a melody
something sweet, plaintive, churchy
lord, something something
something something your people, o lord

82   and they'd pause in what they were doing
to wonder
where they could possibly
have picked that up

St. Febronia

Fourth century nun. Arrested in Nisibis, Mesopotamia during the Diocletian persecution. Many modern hagiographers believe the story of her suffering is fictitious, but she is nevertheless revered in both Eastern and Western churches. According to her legend, she was ordered to renounced Christianity and give up her vow of chastity to marry a Roman soldier. When she refused, she was reportedly subjected to such horrific tortures, the crowd of onlookers begged the commander to stop. She was eventually beheaded.

during my dismemberment
the women in the crowd
        feeling in their own bodies
        every wound inflicted on mine
fell to the ground
screaming
writhing

some of the men too
a few

the rest of them
watched
they didn't want to
knew they shouldn't
tried to turn away
        but turned back
tried to keep their eyes closed
        but opened them again
sickened
ashamed
excited
feeling the torturer's blade
        singing in their moist trembling fingers

the pile of my body parts grew
breasts
hands
feet
teeth
skin
and still they watched
all eyes

these were not bad men
        just naive
believing once it was over
        they would simply forget
never suspecting
        the scene of my mutilation
        was seared into their brains
        and would reappear every time
they caressed their lover's breast
held their daughter's hand
kissed their baby's toes

and every night
they would wake up
shrieking the executioner's song

St. Columba of Sens

Born 257, Spain. Died 273. At age sixteen, Columba fled Spain for Sens, Gaul (today France) to escape the persecution of the Christians under Aurelian. However, she was eventually arrested and imprisoned in Sens and condemned to die. According to her legend, as she awaited her execution, a prison guard attempted to rape her, but was instead himself attacked by a bear that had escaped from a nearby amphitheatre. Later, when she was about to be burned at the stake, a sudden rainfall put out the flames and once again she was left unharmed. She was finally beheaded.

rescued from rape
        by a bear
saved from the flames
        by heaven's own dew

you can see where i'd get the wrong idea

i mounted the steps of the scaffold
        with smug confidence
convinced miracles always come in threes
and that the axe would mysteriously melt away
        in the executioner's hands
or splinter
against my suddenly steely spine

imagine

my

surprise

St. Maria Goretti

Born 1890, Italy. Died 1902. Stabbed by a field worker who lived with her family. Canonized less than 50 years later. First time the Catholic Church bestows the title of martyr on one who did not die for her faith, but in the defence of her virginity. Often depicted wearing a white robe.

88

my martyr's robe
pure white
incorrupt
inviolate
drenched in a rage of blood
          from my breasts, my back, my belly

look
there's my lung
a bit of bone
a glisten of intestine

my body penetrated
fourteen times
but my virginity
untouched

a miracle

some would say

St. Faith

Dates uncertain. Refused to sacrifice to the Roman gods and was burned to death on a grill. According to the legend, as she lay dying, the air around her became thick with a miraculous snow, so her modesty might be preserved during her martyrdom.

it's not that i wasn't grateful
for the snow
i just thought
it would have been an even greater miracle
if the snow had actually extinguished the fire
cooled the grill
saved my life
now *that* would have been a miracle

still and all
as i told god
i appreciated the lovely white swirling curtain
a shroud against shame
defence against the final humiliation

but god just smiled
and shook his head

the snow
i learned
had nothing to do with me

it was to protect the men
all those fine young bucks
who had gathered to witness
a pretty girl slowly roast to death
who elbowed each other
licked their lips and winked
every time she moaned and screamed
who secretly hoped the spectacle
would not be over too soon
as it had been a slow afternoon
and would be hours yet until supper

yes
it was the men
who needed to be protected
shielded
lest a glimpse of my naked nipples
lead them to thoughts of sin

Sts. Justa and Rufina

Third century saints and sisters, Seville, Spain. According to legend, the sisters made pottery for a living, but one day they refused to sell to the townspeople for a celebration honouring the goddess Venus. This so enraged the mob that they smashed all their wares, whereupon the sisters destroyed the idol of Venus. They were brought before the city prefect and ordered to renounce their faith. When they refused, they were tortured and executed. Justa died first, on the rack. Rufina was later strangled to death.

your spirit still sings to me
sweet sister
from the pools of your blood on the floor
the spatters on the cold stone walls
i feel your presence
like the pain of a phantom limb

why do you linger here?
is your heavenly mansion not quite ready for you
or have you come back
to save me?

let me guess

death has bestowed on you
the gift of omniscience
and now you know of your sister's
secret sacrilegious sentiments

yes
i have doubts
do you shudder to hear me speak of it?
does it offend you, dear sister
you of the unassailable certitude?

i trembled when you smashed their little idol
nearly wept when you ordered me
to trample it underfoot
stomp her into the ground

a god
who looks like us, justa!
such a wonder
i wanted to kneel
to kiss
though it would be
an unforgiveable sin

like eve
naked and unashamed
i had hoped
such a god would understand
the troubles of women

no scowl of reproach on her countenance
no darkened brow
no lightning bolts at the ready
her hands were open
wide and friendly

she would not demand the blood sacrifice of her followers
would not insist her children
stretch themselves on crosses
and embrace suffering as though it were salvation

goddess of love, justa!
and pleasure
and why shouldn't love
be pleasurable
why shouldn't the feminine
be divine?

oh don't worry, sister
tomorrow i die for christ
and as they crush my throat
i promise i'll make you proud
not a single hiss of heresy
will escape my obedient lips

but
when my passion is done
and i am closing my eyes for the last time in this world
i will offer a silent prayer
though it damn me
that when i open them again
i will be in her arms

St. Felicity

Third century saint. Martyred in Carthage during the persecution under the Emperor Severus with her mistress Perpetua, a noblewoman, who had recently given birth. Felicity was advanced in her own pregnancy when arrested, and feared she would not be martyred with the others, as pregnant women could not be killed in the arena. However, she was delivered of a daughter shortly before the final day of the games and died along with the rest. The two women are typically pictured together.

oh yes
it's all about her, isn't it?
always has been
always will be
world without end
amen

perpetua, perpetua, perpetua
perpetually perpetua
perpetua in perpetuity

find   one icon
           one painting
           one image
of me
           without her
me
           alone
felicity
           just felicity

they call me
           her companion
           her maid

how sweet

i was her slave

she bought me
she owned me

i was her property

i spent my life
cleaning up after her

obeying her every command
       without question
       without hesitation

she married
she gave me permission to marry
she became pregnant
       and wanted a playmate for her child
i was bred soon afterward
she found religion
unthinkable i would not follow
she was imprisoned
well, i was never free

which is not to say
       she wasn't a good mistress

i was fed
and clothed
and never beaten
without cause

she even acted as my midwife
       when i bore my child
in our prison cell
she let me see my daughter
       wrapped up in her arms
before she gave her away
       to a good home
like an unwanted kitten

after that
nothing mattered

they say i was happy
      to be slaughtered
      along with the rest of them
and that much they got right
it was a relief
not to be left behind
to clean up
one more of her messes

St. Edith Stein

Born 1891, Cologne, Germany. Died 1942, Auschwitz. Brilliant Jewish scholar, teacher and philosopher, she converted to Catholicism and entered the Carmelite monastery in Cologne. With the advent of war, she transferred to the Carmel in Holland, but was arrested after the Nazi invasion of that country. She died in Auschwitz concentration camp at the age of 51. Photographs show her in the brown habit of her order.

(Note: Unknown to the prisoners, many of them had already been selected for execution upon their arrival at Auschwitz. To ensure they would remain calm, these prisoners were given a scrap of soap and told they were to take a shower before further processing. They did not know the shower room was in fact a gas chamber.)

they rejected my name in christ
teresa benedicta of the cross
checked the name
        stein, edith
then crossed it off their list

they stripped away my beautiful habit
the deep soft brown of
sun-warmed earth
sleeves
as wide as the love of god

confiscated the rosary
        that used to shoot off blessings
        from every bead
like the fires of a pinwheel

ripped away my scapular
        my promise of a happy death

what was left…
evidently jewish enough for them

they pressed me
        into the shower room
        with my new community
the congregation of the naked
the sisterhood of soap

and i wondered

what is the proper response
when the spigot above your head
        isn't dripping water
but hissing
        with the wheezy laughter of an old man

what should one do
under these circumstances

believe
hell is god's summer home
and stop
holding your breath

St. Lucy

Born 283. Martyred 304. According to legend, Lucy's mother had arranged for her to marry a pagan official. After Lucy convinced her mother to let her live as a consecrated virgin, she distributed her dowry to the poor, much to the outrage of her jilted fiancé who denounced her to the governor of Syracuse. She was sentenced to a brothel, but when they tried to take her, she could not be moved, even with a team of oxen. She was finally tortured and executed. She is sometimes pictured holding a plate displaying a pair of eyes, as it was thought the gouging out of her eyes was among the tortures she endured. Other legends have it that she gouged them out herself and sent them to a suitor who once praised their charm, in exchange for being left alone.

oh please

yes, i gouged out my own eyes
but not to teach some silly suitor a lesson

i did it because i knew
          what they do
          to women who
          say no to
          powerful men

i thought
          if i can't see
          they can't make me afraid

i thought
          if i have no eyes
          they can't make me cry

small victories

Sts. Valentina And Thea

Dates uncertain. Arrested together during the reign of Galerius (305-311) and brought before the Roman governor Firmillian at Caesarea. When ordered to sacrifice to the gods, it is said Valentina overturned the altar in an act of defiance. She was bound to her companion Thea and together they were burned alive.

they bound us together
        breast to breast
        belly to belly
        thigh to thigh
our women's arms
a shelter for each other

i watched as they added green branches to the wood
        to slow down the fire
        make it last

don't look at them, thea
        she said
look at me
only me
and i fell into the mercy of her eyes

my body trembled
she thought i was afraid
we'll be in heaven soon
        she said
and i bent my head
        to her innocent neck

heaven is this
        i replied
heaven
        is this

Afterword

St. Agatha

St. Agatha

*Born third century, Sicily. Martyred circa 251. Her legend has
it that she was arrested for being a Christian and brought before
the Roman governor of Sicily, Quintianus. When she rebufffed his
seductions, he had her imprisoned, tortured and eventually executed.
His tortures included the tearing off of her breasts, which, it is said,
were miraculously restored to her through a vision of St. Peter
shortly before her martyrdom. She is therefore frequently portrayed
holding a plate bearing a pair of amputated breasts.*

i never asked him for my breasts

too many men already
haggling over my flesh
what stays
what goes

he appeared in my cell
in a great swirl of mystic light
but his eyes stayed glued
to the bloody blanket
lying flat against my chest

bad day? he asked
been better, i replied

here
let me fix you
and he reached out his hand

no thanks
i'm good

a wrinkle creased his saintly brow

but i can give them back to you

i know
but don't

why not?

because i'm asking

he scratched his saintly scalp

but you don't want to enter heaven…
incomplete
do you?

peter
they're going to kill me tomorrow
breasts or no
i'm going in the ground

he worked his saintly jaw
like he was chewing it over
then he nodded
and faded

but he must have been impressed
must have understood

because in the morning
when i could bring myself
to look beneath the covers
i found on my chest
       not my breasts
but his balls